Music Comes in All Siz

Alan Fraser · Illustrated by Beata Szpura

Contents

Rigby®
A Harcourt Achieve Imprint

www.Rigby.com
1-800-531-5015

Music Makers

"What's wrong?" asked Mom as Clara sadly got into the family minivan with her violin case.

"Well, I tried out for orchestra today, and Mr. Martin is making me play the violin," said Clara.

"What's wrong with the violin?" asked Mom.

"Nothing if you want to play classical music the rest of your life. But I want to play jazz, and I was hoping that he would assign me the double bass," said Clara.

"He probably thought that the violin suited your size better. But if you want to play the double bass, then you should ask Mr. Martin if you can switch instruments," offered Mom.

"It couldn't hurt to ask," said Clara.

That night Clara fell asleep listening to a jazz quartet CD that her mother had bought for her. In addition to her jazz CD collection, her dad had already helped her download more than fifty jazz songs onto her MP3 player.

As Mom was driving Clara to school the next day, Clara explained her plan. "I have a whole speech that will convince Mr. Martin that size does not matter when it comes to music," said Clara.

"Great! I can't wait to hear how it goes," said Mom.

During the school day, Clara practiced the speech she had prepared for Mr. Martin. When school ended, she went to orchestra practice. Mr. Martin announced that there would be some changes to the instruments that kids were assigned. Clara waited nervously.

"As I was watching students leave from school with their instruments yesterday, I noticed that Billy had some trouble fitting the double bass, along with three brothers, into the car," said Mr. Martin. "Now Billy would like to switch to a smaller instrument. Does anyone have any suggestions?"

Clara's heart was racing. This was the moment she had been waiting for, and she didn't even have to give her speech. She just had to raise her hand.

The orchestra kids were silent.

Clara's hand flew into the air. "Mr. Martin, Mr. Martin, I have always wanted to play the double bass, and our family has a minivan. And I don't have any brothers or sisters."

The class started giggling because they thought the double bass was more suited to Billy's large frame, not Clara's tiny one.

"Clara, I had no idea that you wanted to play the double bass. Are you sure?" Mr. Martin asked.

"I have never wanted anything more, Mr. Martin," Clara said quickly.

"Well then, Billy and Clara, you are welcome to switch," Mr. Martin said.

After practice Billy helped Clara to her mom's minivan with her new double bass.

"Thank you for your help, Billy," said Clara.

"Thanks for switching with me, Clara," said Billy gratefully.

During practice the next day, Mr. Martin commented on how well the orchestra was doing. "I just wanted to let everyone know how proud I am of your progress. And I also wanted to tell you what I learned from Billy and Clara."

"What's that?" asked Clara.

"Well, I learned that beautiful music comes in all sizes," Mr. Martin said with a smile.

Tiny Tunes

Music Through the Years

In 1877 Thomas Edison made the first recording of a human voice. He recorded "Mary Had a Little Lamb" on a tinfoil record player. That was just the beginning of recorded music.

Since then, music and how we listen to it has kept changing.

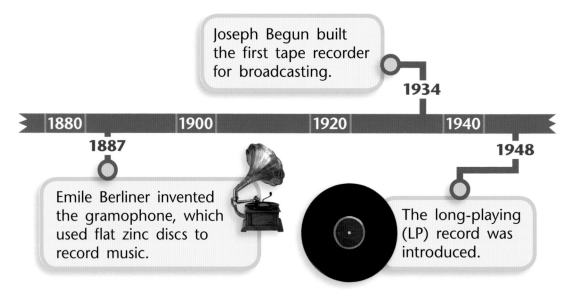

Joseph Begun built the first tape recorder for broadcasting.

1934

1880   1900   1920   1940

1887

1948

Emile Berliner invented the gramophone, which used flat zinc discs to record music.

The long-playing (LP) record was introduced.

Did you know that your parents did not grow up listening to music the way you do? And your parents did not listen to music the way their parents did, either.

By looking at the time line below, can you figure out how your parents and grandparents listened to music when they were your age?

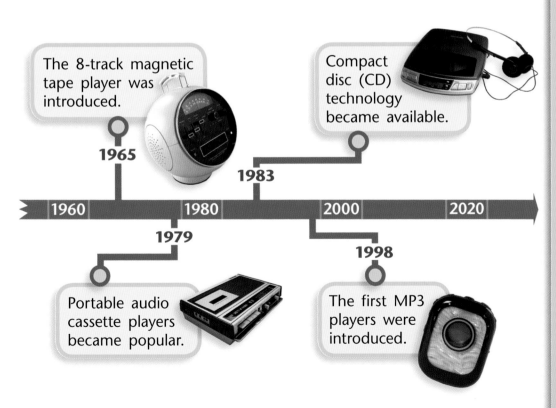

The 8-track magnetic tape player was introduced.

Compact disc (CD) technology became available.

1965

1983

| 1960 | 1980 | 2000 | 2020 |

1979

1998

Portable audio cassette players became popular.

The first MP3 players were introduced.

15

What is an MP3 player?

An MP3 player fits in the palm of your hand, carries thousands of songs, and is one of the newest ways to enjoy music through headphones or speakers. The MP3 player reduces the amount of **bytes** in a song without changing the way the song sounds.

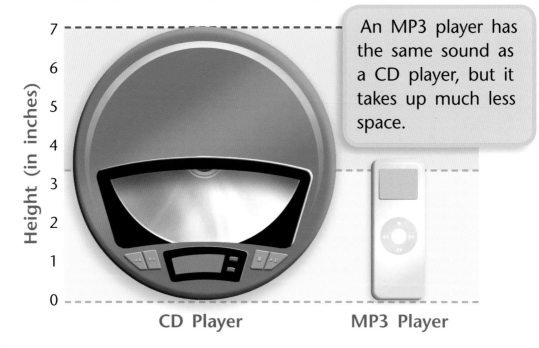

An MP3 player has the same sound as a CD player, but it takes up much less space.

Height (in inches)

7
6
5
4
3
2
1
0

CD Player   MP3 Player

How MP3 Players Work

When you download music onto an MP3 player, the music file gets **compressed**. When you want to listen to your music files, the MP3 player **decompresses** the file so that it is usable. Then the MP3 player changes the file into audio signals. The **amplifier** reads these audio signals and produces sound waves, which are what you hear as music.

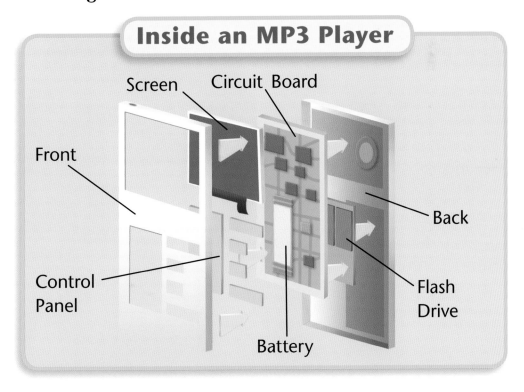

Inside an MP3 Player

Screen Circuit Board

Front

Back

Control Panel

Flash Drive

Battery

What's Your Style?

MP3 players are not all the same. People can choose different players based on how they will use them.

MiniDisc MP3 Players

These players are perfect for people who need to have a lot of storage space. MiniDiscs can handle up to 45 hours of music. They are also great for people who want to store and transfer computer files.

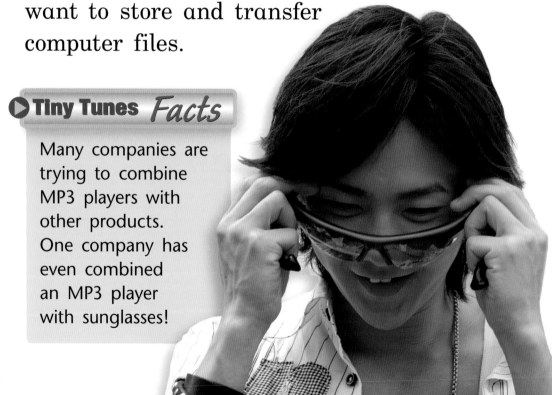

▶ Tiny Tunes Facts

Many companies are trying to combine MP3 players with other products. One company has even combined an MP3 player with sunglasses!

Flash Memory Players

These are the smallest and lightest players. They store much less than the others. But they are good for active people and joggers!

Hard Drive Players

These players are bigger than flash memory players, and they can store an entire music collection. This type of player also uses more battery power.

Plugged in!

Learning

Imagine if you were able to use an MP3 player at school. For some kids, this is already a reality! Students can download a recording of their favorite book read by the actual author, or they can listen to a news broadcast. Students learning foreign languages can even listen to hours of recorded native voices, too.

Students can charge their MP3 batteries at a docking station like this.

Some students podcast as part of their learning.

Many teachers have begun using MP3 players for **podcasting**. Read the following letter from one student to another about her podcasting experiences.

Dear Ashley,

Hooray! Today we started podcasting. We get to record our group plays and speeches into an MP3 player with a microphone. Then we download the recording into the school computer so that other kids can listen to it. It's really cool!

Your friend,

Gina

Traveling

Imagine going to a foreign country and having a tour guide with you at all times. Audio tours can be downloaded from Web sites onto your MP3 player. When you arrive at your destination, you can put on your headphones, walk around, and learn about the sights you're seeing.

Many museums also offer MP3 audio guides. You can download an audio tour of the museum onto your own MP3 player and learn about everything you see as you walk around.

An MP3 player can guide you through a new city.

Glossary

amplifier something that increases the strength of a sound

bytes a basic unit of memory storage

compress to press together into a smaller space

decompress to free from being pressed into a smaller space

podcasting sharing homemade MP3 files

Index